J. Cotter Morison

**Madame de Maintenon**

J. Cotter Morison

**Madame de Maintenon**

ISBN/EAN: 9783743341913

Manufactured in Europe, USA, Canada, Australia, Japa

Cover: Foto ©Thomas Meinert / pixelio.de

Manufactured and distributed by brebook publishing software
(www.brebook.com)

J. Cotter Morison

**Madame de Maintenon**

# MADAME

## DE

# MAINTENON;

## AN ÉTUDE

### BY

### J. COTTER MORISON.

*NEW YORK:*

*Scribner and Welford,* 743 & 745, *Broadway.*

This Edition of MADAME DE MAINTENON is printed with my authorization and approval.

J. COTTER MORISON.

# Madame de Maintenon.[1]

## I.

THE law of the old French monarchy which excluded women from direct inheritance of the
throne, by no means excluded them from great and

---

[1] A singular ill-fortune has attended Madame de Maintenon's
literary remains. The task of publishing her letters in the first
instance fell into the hands of an adventurer of some talent and
more impudence—Laurent Angliviel de la Beaumelle. His
edition, several times reprinted in the eighteenth century, has
been accepted as fairly trustworthy down to recent times ; the
more so as he was known to have been assisted by the ladies of
St. Cyr, who furnished him with valuable original documents.
It now appears that his edition teems with forgeries of the most
flagitious kind. He not only tampered with the text of genuine
letters, often actually re-writing them and interpolating fraudu-
lent additions of his own, but he forged whole letters by the
dozen whenever unwelcome gaps in the authentic correspondence

often

often paramount influence in affairs of State. Indeed
it would not be difficult to show that in few European
countries has female authority been more frequent

suggested or permitted the deception. The almost incredible
extent of his imposture was only exposed when the late M.
Théophile Lavallée commenced his edition of Madame de
Maintenon's general correspondence. M. Lavallée had himself
been a dupe, like all preceding writers, of La Beaumelle's men-
dacity. About twenty years ago the need of a new and critical
edition of Madame de Maintenon's letters and other works was
much felt, and two editors devoted themselves to the task, in-
dependently and in ignorance of each other's labours, the Duc
de Noailles and M. Lavallée. M. Guizot brought them into
communication, and M. Lavallée was charged with the whole
undertaking. Unhappily, he has died before completing his
task, only four volumes having appeared of his edition of the
Letters, which was intended to comprise ten.

M. Lavallée had a *culte* for Madame de Maintenon, and his
work, extending over twelve years, devoted to her memory, was
truly a labour of love. He disinterred autograph letters, whenever they had been preserved, and accepted only such copies as
were guaranteed by being transcriptions from the originals made
by the ladies of St. Cyr. It was on confronting these authentic
documents with La Beaumelle's edition that the magnitude of

                                                          and

and predominant than in the country which boasted the Salic law. Whether as indigenous mistresses or imported queens, women shaped the policy and

---

the latter's fraud was first brought fully to light. It is not too much to say that Madame de Maintenon has been hitherto chiefly known and painted on the faith of this unscrupulous inventor. Even the best and most recent books are filled with his fabrications ; *e.g.* Henri Martin, in his elaborate and painstaking "History of France," quotes almost exclusively the apocryphal letters ; expressions as familiar as household words, supposed to be Madame de Maintenon's, are now proved to be fictions of La Beaumelle's. For instance, the famous sentences, "Je le renvoie toujours affligé, jamais désespéré," "Cela m'engage à approuver des choses fort opposées à mes sentiments," etc., etc., are not Madame de Maintenon's at all, though it is difficult to banish them from the mind. As M. Lavallée says, it will take a long time before the false impression created by La Beaumelle's imposture is dispelled, if it ever is entirely.

Of course, we have to take M. Lavallée's word for these statements. But I believe his honourable character has never been doubted, and his work proves him to have been a most painstaking and well-informed editor. When I quote Madame de Maintenon's letters, it is to his edition I refer, except when otherwise indicated.

wielded

wielded the power of the French kings to a degree
which could not be easily matched in any other royal
house of Europe.   During considerable periods of
French history the titular king is a shadow, and
the foreground of politics is occupied by a vigorous
queen (regent or consort), or an ambitious con-
cubine.   From Blanche of Castile and Agnes Sorel,
to Madame de Pompadour and Marie Antoinette,
French politics repeatedly fell into feminine hands.
The result was not often fortunate for France.
Although that country has perhaps produced as
many eminent women as the rest of Europe put
together, it has not been happy in its female rulers.
We look in vain through its annals for any woman
on or near the throne that can be compared with
Isabella of Spain, Elizabeth of England, or Maria
Theresa of Austria.   The most beautiful and lofty
female character in all history, does indeed belong
to French politics; but the incomparable maid of
Domremy

Domremy was far from any legitimate or illegitimate connection with the throne. In all despotic monarchies the too frequent accident of a weak and uxorious prince leads naturally to the domination of intriguing women and courtly parasites. The foreign queens, or the beauties of native growth who supplant them, have rarely much inducement to make a magnanimous use of their power. That women are capable in a high degree of the sentiment of patriotism, will be denied only by the uncandid or the ignorant. But the Salic law excluded from Government precisely those women who by birth and education would have been most likely to be inspired by that noble passion. Anne de Beaujeu showed that a French king's daughter could be far more worthy to bear rule than her brother, the King's son. There were imperial qualities in la Grande Mademoiselle, which might make us wish that her lofty, if also somewhat fantastic daring, had found a

fitter

fitter theatre than the grotesque tragi-comedy of the Fronde.

Among the women who have left a lasting name and mark in French history, Madame de Maintenon undoubtedly holds a prominent if not a chief place. The length of her reign, and the durability of her influence, are without parallel. As Louis XIV. reigned longer than any other king of France, so Madame de Maintenon occupied the position of chief favourite for a longer period than anyone before or after her. Her extraordinary career, during which she travelled from the lowest depths of poverty and obscurity to the loftiest place but one in Europe, has struck the imagination and curiosity both of contemporaries and posterity. Her exalted, but to the end ambiguous position, had the same effect, and contributed to endow her with that air of mystery of which few minds escape the fascination. She herself said she should be an enigma to posterity, and she

seems

seems rather to have liked the reflection than otherwise. The object at once of unbounded adulation
and unscrupulous calumny, reserved and self-con-
tained to the verge of duplicity, she has left a
reputation which to this day remains in the half-light
which partakes of legend. Two legends concerning
her had commenced before her death,—one highly
flattering, the other as hostile. According to one,
she was an apparition well-nigh or quite miraculous,
a sort of courtly Joan of Arc, divinely appointed to
convert a licentious king from his immoral ways;
according to the other, she was a miracle of crafty
intrigue, who, with a subtlety hardly human, had
bewitched an aged monarch into humiliating sub-
jection to her. We are not reduced to a random
guess that the truth probably lies between these two
extremes. Enough remains in her own handwriting
(though it is conjectured that she destroyed nine-
tenths of her correspondence) to show us that she
was

was equally removed from the angelic character, whether dark or light. The pretension of her unreserved admirers, past and present, that all her actions were inspired by a pure and lofty piety, that she submitted for years to a court life of hot intrigue in a company the least virtuous from motives of perfect virtue, can only be met by a smile. The pretension of her unreserved enemies, that she with forecasting insight played, without conscience or scruple, her deep game of hypocrisy and ambition for the sake of worldly honour, can only be met in the same way. Madame de Maintenon in this respect has only received the common measure of justice and injustice which usually falls to those who attain extraordinary pre-eminence after starting from relatively lowly beginnings. The ambitious climber to the giddy height is credited with a profound plan of operations from the first, with a distinct view of the distant goal ultimately reached, but designed all along, and with the

the artifice and cunning needed to secure the stages which led to it. The end of the career is supposed to explain its commencement. The earliest steps were taken in reference to the path along which the last were meant to fall. It is thus that Cæsar is supposed to have set out to conquer Gaul with the settled intention of conquering the Senate afterwards, and Cromwell to have entered the Long Parliament with the matured purpose of bringing Charles I. to the scaffold. Such conceptions are wanting in imaginative grasp and reality. They suppose that human life can be written out like a well-conned play, and that the dim future years can be seen through and fitted with appropriate stage directions. Inapplicable to the most audacious and inventive schemers for power, this notion is peculiarly misplaced with regard to Madame de Maintenon. Few of her equals in ability and force of character have had so little ideal lift of spirit, or of an eye far-
reaching,

reaching, and bent on distant horizons. Less than most was she given to building castles in the air, or to regarding as present what still lay hidden in the womb of the future. On the contrary, her success and her strength lay in her complete sobriety of temper, and a patience that could not be wearied. If she could have foreseen her career it is probable she would never have attempted it. Not soaring genius, but consummate common-sense was her quality. It was far less ambition than the most watchful prudence that directed her steps, and both prudence and common-sense would have dissuaded her from a path which she ultimately trod without a fall.

Frances d'Aubigné, afterwards Madame Scarron and Marquise de Maintenon, came of an ancient family originally from Anjou. None of her ancestors were distinguished except her grandfather, the famous Agrippa d'Aubigné, the friend and companion in

arms

arms of Henry IV., and one of the most strenuous and original characters of the sixteenth century. One of the fathers of French prose and a copious writer of vigorous verse, he was also one of the most fierce and intrepid warriors of that wild time. He was presented to Henry as a man " who found nothing too hot for him," and he proved the correctness of the character abundantly, especially by saving Henry's life at the risk of his own. The valiant old Huguenot had a most unworthy son named Constant d'Aubigné, a depraved and feeble libertine, who was twice saved from the gallows by his father's influence. But the foolish creature, not content with spending his substance, and committing rape and murder, conspired against Cardinal Richelieu, for which he was imprisoned for many years, and only released by the Cardinal's death. Constant had for second wife (he had killed his first) Jeanne de Cardilhac, a brave woman, but soured by her trials and

and domestic unhappiness. She went to share her scandalous husband's prison at Niort, and there, in the extreme of privation, she gave birth, 27th November, 1635, to a girl, who afterwards became Madame de Maintenon.[1]

Frances had a wretched childhood, the gloom and misery of which were never effaced from her mind. Her mother went to Paris, and lived there in extreme poverty, in pursuit of hopeless lawsuits. Her abandoned father persevered in his vices. Her early years were tended by a paternal aunt, Madame de Villette, for whom, to the end of her life, she retained the most affectionate memory. At length a brighter prospect seemed to open before the unfortunate family. The French of the seventeenth century were not so unable or unwilling to emigrate

---

[1] " La famille d'Aubigné et l'enfance de Madame de Maintenon," p. 77, par Théophile Lavallée.

**as**

as they have since become, and Constant d'Aubigné,
now sixty years old, solicited and obtained the post
of Governor of Marie-Galante, situate in Martinique.
The exiles sailed a family of five, the father, mother,
two boys, and a girl, the latter, Frances, not quite ten
years old. On the voyage Frances sickened even
unto apparent death. She was about to be buried
in the sea, when her mother insisted on once more
seeing her child, and finding the heart's action had
not stopped, she declared that her daughter was not
dead, and saved her from the deep. It was a narrow
escape. The cannon was already charged, to be fired
as she dropped into the ocean, when her mother's im-
portunity rescued her. The fact is the more singular,
as Jeanne d'Aubigné seems to have been a harsh
unloving mother. Her daughter said she had never
been kissed by her but twice in her life. It is probable that maternal coldness was assisted by religious
estrangement. Her aunt, Madame de Villette, was,
like

like her father Agrippa, a staunch Huguenot, and had
brought up Frances in her own faith ; but her mother
was a Catholic.    Once when she took her to mass the
little Calvinist turned her back to the altar, for which
her ears were boxed ; but she bore the punishment
with pride, and gloried in suffering for her religion.

The Martinique adventure did not prosper.    Constant d'Aubigné remained an incurable spendthrift to
the end.    Though in want of means, he yet gave his
wife a staff of twenty-four slaves to wait upon her.
At the end of two years he died, and his widow and
children at once returned to France.    Again Frances
tasted the bitterness of dependence, and the cold
welcome of indifferent relations.    She fell into the
custody of a Madame de Neuillant, an aunt by marriage, who made her a mere drudge in her farm-
yard, set her to mind her poultry, and shod her with
sabots.    The religious difficulty again came up, and
she was both coaxed and coerced towards a change
of

of faith. Her precocious shrewdness was by this time enlightened as to the position of a Huguenot in France, and her conversion to Catholicism seems to have been a smooth and easy business. In her seventeenth year she met the burlesque writer, Paul Scarron.

Scarron, though barely past middle age, was a helpless cripple, having only the use of "his right hand, his eyes, and his tongue." But his indomitable vivacity triumphed over his bodily infirmities, and he was regarded as one of the brightest wits and authors of his time. His writings belong to a school as antiquated and forgotten in French literature as the writings of Lilly and Cowley are in ours. They have that perverted ingenuity and laborious pleasantry which seem to us so dreary. There are few less amusing books than his once famous " Roman Comique." Yet Scarron found an ardent admirer in the great Racine, and in any case his house was

B                                                        the

the resort of the most approved wit and fashion of
Paris. Frances d'Aubigné's forlorn condition touched
the kind heart of the afflicted joker, and he offered
her either to pay her entrance fee in a good convent,
or marriage. She chose the latter alternative. She
was less than half his age, and though called his
wife, was never anything but his nurse. In spite of
his maladies, Scarron kept open house, and the company, though distinguished by rank and intelligence,
was free, not to say licentious, in conversation. The
demure matron of seventeen was at once put upon
her mettle, and she soon showed the stuff of which
she was made. In three months she had banished
all indecorum from her husband's table, and so im-
pressed his companions with her worth and dignity,
that one of them said if he were offered the choice
of behaving in an unbecoming manner to the Queen
(Anne of Austria) or to her, he would prefer doing so
to the Queen. With that she was a tender helpmeet,

not

not only ruling his household, but assisting him in his literary work. For eight years the strange union lasted with mutual satisfaction. At his death, Scarron said he had but one regret, that he was unable to leave his wife better off than he did. He indeed left her little but debts. Only a few weeks before his death an incident occurred of singular irony. On August 26th, 1660, Louis XIV. entered Paris with all the pomp which the court and the capital could command, on the occasion of his marriage with his young queen, Maria Theresa of Spain. Paris had never seen such a show. The nobles and the municipal authorities vied with each other in lavish magnificence, and the procession lasted through the long hours of a summer's day. Madame Scarron witnessed it as an obscure spectator, and wrote an account of it to a friend. "Nothing," she says to her correspondent, "nothing I or anyone could say could give you an idea of the magnificent spectacle ;

tacle; nothing could surpass it." Twenty-four years afterwards Madame Scarron herself, after a marriage service carefully concealed, celebrated by night in the palace of Versailles, became the young queen's successor.[1]

On Scarron's death, she had again to face the world without resources. But now she had made influential friends, and she presently procured a pension from the Queen Mother. It was small, but Madame Scarron was a mistress of thrift and economical resource. Her inexpensive and simple attire was not without a certain grave *coquetterie*, and she was careful to be *bien chaussée*. Her remarkable beauty—she was generally called *la belle Indienne*—the charm of her manner and conversation, caused her company to be eagerly sought after. But she had another gift more adapted than these to make her friendship valued,

---

[1] "Correspondance Générale," vol. i. p. 72.

and

and that was a power of rendering herself infinitely serviceable to all whom she approached. Trained in the hard school of adversity, her natural endowment as a *ménagère* had been developed to a supreme degree. No household that had once received Madame Scarron, but missed and regretted her when she left it. In the drawing-room, the kitchen, or the sickroom, she was equally pleasing and unobtrusively useful : but in the nursery, her innate love of children, and skill in their management, made her presence almost indispensable. In rendering these offices, she never spared trouble or pains. On one occasion she nursed an old lady for three months without leaving the house. On another, she not only took charge of Madame de Montchevreuil's house and children, but attended to the sale of the farm-stock as well. When one of her friends got married, the whole preparation of the wedding devolved upon her. It is easy to understand that such a woman was welcome and

popula:,

popular, and what a valuable education she thus
acquired for her subsequent career.

Madame Scarron's virtue is not so exhausted a
topic in France as the similar one concerning Queen
Elizabeth is in England. It is still discussed with
some vivacity by her blind admirers and blind detractors, who seem to have inherited the passions of
her friends and foes in the palace of Versailles. St.
Simon's calumnies against her are still accepted, or
laid aside with only partial sincerity, by the one;
on the other hand, the reverence felt for her by her
novices at St. Cyr, does not seem excessive or un-
warranted to the others. The unprejudiced inquirer
will agree with Ste. Beuve that the evidence against
her correctness of conduct is not worth attending to.
The fact that she was acquainted, not intimate, with
Ninon de l'Enclos, a friend of her husband, has
been made the ground of the most injurious infer-
ences and statements. The animosity of her enemies
has

has blinded them to consistency of character. Every trustworthy record proves that Madame de Maintenon moved in a plane which diverged at right angles from the path which leads to sins of the flesh. It was not that she resisted such temptations; she was not aware of them. It was her favourite maxim that an irreproachable behaviour is also the cleverest, in a worldly sense. She acknowledged that a wish to stand well with the world, and win its esteem, was her master passion, and that "she *hated* everything that could expose her to contempt." Her clear and subtle intellect grew out of a soil covered with snow. She owned that it was not out of love that she sedulously nursed her sick friend for three months, but in order to acquire a good reputation. It would be ungenerous to construe this avowal against her too literally. If not warm, she was singularly constant in her affections, and longsuffering even to timidity. Setting aside her religious principles, of which none but

but the uncandid will dispute the persistency, even if
they deny their fervour, it is evident that in her cool,
sedate mind, the impulses in question found no place.
Far greater and richer would she have been if they
had.   Her lips were never touched with fire, and no
flame, holy or unholy, ever burned in the depths of
her heart.

For about ten years Madame Scarron, after her
husband's death, led an agreeable life in the most
refined circles of Parisian society.   She was on terms
of intimacy with Madame de Sévigné, who was struck
with the mingled amiability and accuracy of her mind.
They supped every night together, and Madame de
Sévigné pronounced her company " delicious."   It
was in these circumstances that a proposition was
made to her (the exact date is not known—probably
in 1670) which gave a new direction to her fortunes,
and one very different from anything she could have
expected.   She was asked to take charge of certain
children

children of her friend Madame de Montespan; and their father was rumoured to be no other than the King of France.

We now enter upon a period of her life beset with doubt, obscurity, and legend, through which it is difficult to see one's way to trustworthy fact. We have the saintly legend on the one hand (which she herself in her latter years carefully propagated), representing her as the pure soul who, from the loftiest motives, entered the corrupt atmosphere of the court, and that by the most suspicious of back doors. On the other side is the legend which exhibits her in a character but little removed from that of a procuress, with an ambition as mean as it was unscrupulous. The situation, and the person who filled it, afford material of singular dramatic interest, in which the play of a subtle and complex character winds and circulates amid circumstances more complex still. Our interest in Madame de Maintenon is quenched as soon as we

regard

regard her exclusively in the light of either legend, either as a woman of guileless sincerity, or as an accomplished intriguer, devoid of all conscience. She derives her peculiar attraction and piquancy precisely from the constant interaction of contending motives of worldly wisdom and spiritual aspiration, between her struggles to secure a high place at court, and a safe, final retreat to the kingdom of heaven. She pursued both ends with an energy which never relented, and showed a tenacity which cannot be surpassed in her resolution to make the best of both worlds.

She met the tempting offer to take charge of the King's natural children with refined diplomacy. With Madame de Montespan's children she said she could have no concern, but if the children in question were indeed the King's, and his Majesty were pleased to lay his commands upon her, she was ready to obey. A widow in narrow circumstances might have been excused

excused if she had shown less self-control and insight in the presence of an offer which promised emolument and a secure future. But Madame Scarron saw to the bottom of the situation at once, and how different would be her position if she were employed by the King, or only by his mistress. The King did lay his commands upon her, and at once, with prompt energy, she took the whole burden of her new office. This burden was no light one. The most complete secrecy was one of the stipulations, and she conformed to it with an exactness which would have done credit to a commissary of police. She was lodged with her young charges in a roomy house in the then remote quarter of the Rue de Vaugirard, but concealed, with an innate genius for dissimulation which could dispense with teaching, her new occupation even from her most intimate friends. With unconscious *naïveté* she boasted in after life of her successful duplicity, and confided to the virgin innocents

ot

of St. Cyr the story of her adroit management
in hiding the results of sin. "Often," she said, "I
passed the whole night watching by the bedside of
one of those children when unwell. I returned home
by a back door in the morning, and, after dressing,
I went out in a carriage from the front door to
the Hôtel d'Albret, or Richelieu, in order that my
usual circle might not suspect that I had any secret
to keep." She frequently went on foot to escape
notice, and carefully disguised, carrying under her
arm clothes, and even food, doing any household
work that presented itself, in preference to admitting
indiscreet strangers.[1]

Not only Christian saintliness but a strong sense of
human dignity might have shrunk from such offices.
We must remember that after all such behaviour was
fairly in accordance with the views of the courtly

---

[1] "Correspondance Générale," vol. i. p. 146.

world

world at the time. Vice was not vice when practised by a king. Madame Colbert had taken charge in a similar way of Mademoiselle de la Vallière's children, and nobody was shocked. Neither is Madame de Maintenon shocked. But her new position brought out prominently, perhaps fully revealed, to herself for the first time the two master motives which guided her through life,—worldly advancement, and salvation in the next world. No one knew better than she that the licentious court of Louis XIV. was about the last place in which a sensitive piety could feel safe or happy. On the other hand, no courtier at St. Germain or Versailles was more determined to push his fortunes by pleasing the King. Hence an inward conflict which required to be quelled. Hence the need of a sophistry to deceive self and others as regarded the impulse which retained her in a position so inconsistent with her principles of religious severity. She knew well that she was envied rather than blamed

blamed for the post she had secured; but she insists
on being pitied for it, strives to make herself and
others believe that she does violence to her feelings
by remaining in it, and that her one anxiety is to get
away. She was much helped in this rather difficult
task by a judicious choice of a confessor, an intelli-
gent toady, the Abbé Gobelin, who was careful to
advise her to do precisely what he saw she wished.
We may well believe that he at an early period
assured her it was her duty to remain at court, however painful it might be. Churchmen in Louis XIV.'s
time knew the value of court favour, and a person so
near the King as the governess of his children was too
valuable a friend to be allowed to indulge in weak
scruples about the spiritual healthiness of the place.
In the first instance the rather slow-witted Louis had
felt a dread of Madame Scarron; her reputation as a
*bel esprit* was a little alarming to his dignity. It was
only through Madame de Montespan's influence that
his

his repugnance was overcome. But when he knew her better and saw her closer a great change took place in his impressions. He discovered that the demure and humble head nurse of his children possessed an intellect which by its culture, delicacy, and penetration eclipsed the boisterous vigour of his mistress. He found his way with increased frequency to her apartment, and seemed to take more pleasure in his visits the oftener they were made. What did these things mean? Though verging on forty, Madame Scarron still retained much of her early beauty, the severity of her morals had long been celebrated, her reprobation of unchastity was notorious. The court, as a microcosm of France, contained a devout party, as well as parties who were by no means devout. These good men, of whom the Duc de Montausier and Bossuet were the recognised chiefs, while reverencing their King to the verge of idolatry, were yet pained beyond expression

by

by his licentious life: his frailty in the presence of
female beauty tarnished in their eyes all the surpassing glories of his reign.   If he could only be
converted to virtuous habits nothing would remain
to be desired; but his inclination to appropriate to
himself the wives of other men was a menacing evil
which threatened to bring the country to ruin.   His
wars and reckless expenditure, and the widespread
misery they caused, were visitations in which piety
saw an Almighty hand.   These were calamities from
which one should pray to be delivered.   But the
King's incontinency was a misfortune far more urgent
and dangerous than any of these.   And yet it was a
difficult subject to approach.   Mascaron, by a ser-
mon of indiscreet zeal on the observance of the
seventh commandment, had drawn upon himself re-
buke and disgrace.   Perhaps the same sentiments
from the mouth of a pretty woman might be better
received.   With whom the thought originated does
not

not appear. But it is certain that the devout party were not long in coming to the conclusion that Madame Scarron might be successfully used as a sort of female missionary to bring about the conversion of the King. Herewith a prospect opened before her beyond the dreams of hope or ambition. All contradictions were reconciled. Piety and patriotism, charity for her neighbour, just pride in her King, all converged to command her to stay at court, to save his soul and make her own fortune.

But although the theory was clear, its application was beset with difficulties. The elements of the problem were complex and not easily co-ordinated. Firstly, there was the large debt of gratitude to Madame de Montespan for her introduction to court. Secondly, there was the King's passion for his mistress still at a high temperature. Thirdly, there were the children to be reared in dutiful reverence to the King, but in a strange ambiguous atti-

c                                                              tude

tude towards their mother. Fourthly, there were the interests of religion which commanded the expulsion of the benefactress, and a thorough reformation of the King's habits. The skill with which Madame Scarron rode these four horses abreast proves her to have been endowed with very extraordinary qualities. She commenced by putting herself in a safe position against any reproaches of the mistress, by exhorting her to a godly life. Loyal friendship, Christian charity, could not do less than warn an erring sister of the danger of her ways. But after this frankness she was free to speak to the King, when opportunity offered, and the ample mantle of religious zeal was more than sufficient to shelter her from all insinuations of ingratitude or self-seeking. ·As regards the children, the obstacles were trifling. Madame Scarron's pure and perfect love of children is one of the most attractive traits in her character. It cost her nothing to win their love from their harsh

and

and imperious mother. Remained the fourth impediment, the King's attachment to his mistress.

No sacred bard, or what would have been much better, no prying, eavesdropping Boswell has painted for us the "terrible scenes" which soon ensued. When it at last became clear to Montespan that her creature, her underling, her drudge, was threatening to become her rival, the explosion of choler, as we may well conceive, was very grand indeed. Pent up together in a narrow space at Versailles or St. Germain, the two ladies were brought into daily, almost hourly, contact. It was a situation to bring out the fighting qualities of tame women, and neither of these was tame, though they differed much in their style of courage. It says a good deal for their self-command that they never came to blows. Once apparently they nearly did, when they suffered themselves to be surprised by the King in a crisis so violent that he found them quite hot with the ardour of of battle. With a simplicity which must have been feigned, he asked what was the matter. Madame Scarron recovered her calm on the instant, and made answer, "If your Majesty will pass into the adjoining apartment, I shall have the honour of telling you."[1] Montespan let them go, choked, we may presume, with floods of rage, bewilderment, and despair. Her soft, feline enemy then unbosomed herself to the King, told of the harshness, the injustice, the cruelty of Madame de Montespan, and struck an attitude, we may depend, in which piety, beauty, and Christian resignation struggled to produce a complete effect. "Have you not remarked," said the King, rather ungallantly, "how her fine eyes fill with tears whenever she hears of a touching and generous action?" It was a churlish question, and must have

---

[1] "Il se passe ici des choses terribles entre Madame de Montespan et moi : le roi en fut hier témoin."—"Correspondance Générale," vol. i. p. 254.—Mém. de Madame de Caylus.

been

been a heavy blow, showing that fine eyes might still be a match for religious love-making, and a menacing hint not to proceed too fast, or attempt to carry matters with a high hand. But Madame de Maintenon's endurance and tenacity of patience was more than equal to the emergency. "I spoke yesterday," she writes to the toady confessor, "to Madame de Montespan, and begged her and the King not to consider any ill-humour I showed as a proof of sulkiness towards them. She and I are again to have a conference this morning. I intend to be very soft in all I say; still I remain firm in the intention to leave them at the end of the year, and I shall employ my time till then in praying God to lead me where it will be best for my salvation."[1] It would no doubt

---

[1] "Je priais le roi et elle de ne point regarder la mauvaise humeur où je leur parraissais comme une bouderie contre eux. . . . Madame de Montespan et moi devons nous parler ce matin : ce sera de ma part avec beaucoup de douceur."—"Correspondance Générale," vol. i. p. 212.

be difficult to draw, with perfect equity, the line here
which separated subtle self-deception from half-con-
scious hypocrisy. That both were present we may
charitably believe—cant and sincerity; or, as Mr.
Carlyle says, "sincere cant." However, men and
women must fight the battle of life with such weapons
as they can command, and neither cant nor sincerity
could be dispensed with in this crisis. With a devout
party anxiously looking on and watching this singular
duel between two strange champions, with an immoral party equally anxious and supporting the cause
of "fine eyes," one could not afford to give points.
All the more reason for making one's own side feel
the value of the services rendered. "I know," she
writes to the useful confessor, " that I can save myself here, but I think I could do it better elsewhere.
I cannot believe it is God's wish that I should suffer
from Madame de Montespan. I have a thousand
times desired to take the vows, and the fear of re-
                                        penting

penting such a step has made me pass over impulses which many would have considered proofs of vocation." The confessor, for once, proved himself a dunce as well as a toady, and began to take her at her word, and hinted belief in her wish to adopt a religious life. She lost no time in undeceiving him. " I have expressed myself badly," she writes, " if you understood that I was thinking of becoming a nun. I am too old to change my position now, and according to the fortune I receive from the King" (she was justly expecting a fitting reward for the trouble she had taken with his children), "I shall set about establishing myself in perfect quietude."[1] Before her brother, less diplomacy was required, and to him she says, "It was thought I had been got rid of here" (at Versailles), "but you who know me will

---

[1] "Je me suis mal expliquée, si vous avez compris que je pense à être religieuse ; je suis trop vieille pour changer de condition."—"Correspondance Générale," vol. i. p. 210.

also

also know that I am not so easily got rid of."[1]
These extracts, taken from her letters written at the
moment, which might be indefinitely multiplied, give
a very different impression from that of the simpering
legend which, long years after, she propagated for the
edification of her novices of St. Cyr, in which she
appears as the meek and miraculous instrument of a
higher power, and touching victim sacrificed to the
needs of State.

At last Montespan's broad moon of favour waned,
narrowed, and disappeared, and Maintenon waxed
brighter than ever in antithetical splendour. Her
unflinching admirers await us here with arguments
they deem demonstrative of her pious and perfect
disinterestedness. Between Montespan's eclipse and
the Queen's death, they ask us how to explain her

---

[1] ". . . l'on crut être défait de nous. Vous croirez bien,
vous qui nous connaissez, que l'on ne s'en défait pas si aisé-
ment."—" Correspondance Générale," vol. i. p. 336.

conduct

conduct except on the hypothesis of her unselfish regard for the King's morals, her devout yearning to make him a model of continency and Christian virtue. The Queen, we are told, declared that under God she owed it to Madame de Maintenon, that after twenty years of neglect her husband began to treat her with kindness. It is supposed that this evidence of Madame de Maintenon's purity of motive cannot be resisted. She could not have foreseen, it is remarked, the Queen's proximate death. She could not, if she had, have aimed at taking her place; and as for taking the place of Montespan, it cannot even be mentioned with propriety. Therefore pure religion, and undefiled by worldly interest, alone impelled her. Is this conclusion quite clear? Let us grant that she reconciled husband and wife. Let her have all the credit which such an achievement deserves. From her point of view it was a triumph fitted to win the applause of angels, and we need not doubt that her good

good work was its own reward.   Let us also loudly
proclaim that her own virtue was impeccable, and
that she would have given her body to be burned,
rather than yield a hair's-breadth to unchastity.   But
was there no other path open along which ambition
could move?   Was there not a place vacant for a
female confessor, or rather was not that place already
admirably filled in the unanimous opinion of the
godly by Madame de Maintenon herself?   And was
it not a place of surpassing honour, and exquisite in
its singularity?   Let us imagine a woman in whom
the vulgar passions are extinct, or rather never ex-
isted : let us suppose her with a strong propensity to a
formal and legal righteousness, who coupled therewith
a deep but wary ambition.   Thus stated, the problem
is as good as solved.   But further, was the Queen a
hindrance, or not rather a valuable instrument in her
hand?   The Queen was not a rival to be feared for a
moment—the poor meek woman who stood in such

awe

awe of the King, that she trembled in every limb when he sent for her unexpectedly. What would have been dangerous was another young mistress of Madame de Montespan type, brilliant and enterprising, who might soon make havoc of the King's good resolutions, and fill the faces of the devout with shame and confusion. But while the Queen lived, and the King remained on good terms with her—and the female confessor who had done so much might be trusted to ensure that— a pledge for his good behaviour was, so to speak, held in hand. So far from being an obstacle, the Queen was a most useful pawn in Madame de Maintenon's game, and we may well believe that her death filled the latter with no slight perturbation. It changed, indeed, the position into a critical phase. Madame de Maintenon's place, beside a widower, was very different from what it had been beside a married man, protected by his wife. Would the newly acquired virtue of the King remain firm ? Policy dissuaded

dissuaded another marriage with some foreign prin-
cess. Another young royal family was not to be
desired in the state of the finances, but no one could
guarantee that one would not arrive, if the King
married again. But what was the alternative?
Madame de Maintenon, we are told, at this time
passed through a period of mental anxiety, very un-
usual to her austere and self-controlled temper. She
not only shed abundant tears, but became so restless
that she roamed in the forest of Fontainebleau, with
a single companion, sometimes even at unseemly
hours. The few letters she wrote at this epoch
reveal profound agitation of spirit. Presently the
clouds break, and she is seen sitting in lofty calm,
radiant with a happiness which she does not explain.
It is probable that during this trying interval the
proposition of her marriage with the King was discussed and decided in the affirmative. We may well
believe that so momentous a decision was not arrived
at

at without aching doubt and hesitation. The exact date of the marriage has never been divulged. All that is known is that probably in June, 1684, seven persons were assembled at midnight in one of the private apartments of the palace of Versailles. These were the King and his bride; Father la Chaise, who said mass; the Archbishop of Paris, who gave the nuptial blessing; Louvois and Montchevreuil, who were witnesses; and Bontemps, the first *valet de chambre*, who prepared the altar and served the mass. The widow of. Paul Scarron had become the actual but unrecognised Queen of France. She was forty-nine, and the King forty-six years of age.

II.

## II.

A PLEASING outline of Madame de Maintenon at the time of her marriage is given by the ladies of St. Cyr: "Her voice was most agreeable and her manner winning; she had a bright and open forehead, a natural gesture of a perfect hand, eyes full of fire, and the carriage of a figure so graceful and supple that it eclipsed the best at court. The first impression she made was imposing, through a veil of severity; but the cloud vanished when she spoke and smiled." Fénélon, a fastidious judge, said she was "Wisdom speaking through the mouth of the Graces," and her arch-enemy, St. Simon, said that she was "grace itself." A striking and attractive presence, no doubt. Her mental endowments have been partly displayed

displayed already—a deep, but by no means irritable
self-esteem, of vanity not a trace, patience insuper-
able, a cool and solid judgment, which took the exact
measure of persons and things, and saw the situation with precise truth, capable, also, of prompt and
vigorous action when required. "I must have mules,"
she wrote to her brother when about to follow the
King in one of his holiday tours among his troops—
"I must have mules, cost what they will. Coaches
upset, or remain stuck in the roads. Mules always
reach their destination." The King should see that
one woman at least could be self-helpful and ener-
getic. When Madame de Brinon—the Mother
Superior she had placed over St. Cyr—lost her head
and became rather noisily insubordinate, a swift *lettre
de cachet* transferred her to another convent—a real
*coup d'état* which set all Paris wondering. And yet
she was placable and incapable of rancour, for all St.
Simon may say. The final impression is that of a
cold

cold over-prudent nature, of which a wary, long-headed selfishness was the chief spring.

Her correspondence with her brother is a marvel of frigid worldly-wise exhortation. In the hundred and odd of her authentic letters to him, which still exist, it is not too much to say that there is not a generous sentiment to be found. Though genuinely anxious for both his spiritual and temporal welfare, she uses a tone so creeping and mean that we cannot wonder at the small effect of her counsel. The burden of nearly every letter is, " Live within your income, and think of your salvation." " Good-bye, my dear brother," she writes ; " we will feast ourselves at Maintenon " (she had just bought the estate) "if God spares us. Nevertheless, think of your soul, and be assured that it is ill-advised not to put one's self in the state one would wish to be in at the hour of death." " We shall meet again, if it please God. Think of Him in order to be always ready to die, and for the restlet us keep
ourselves

ourselves jolly." Security as regards income, and security as regards salvation, are the two points which she never leaves out of sight. And she wants no more than security in either case. Though without a tinge of avarice or greed, as her subsequent career showed, she never rested till she had put the good property of Maintenon between herself and poverty. In the same way, with reference to spiritual affairs, though punctilious about her salvation, she always treats the matter as a sort of prudent investment, a preparation against a rainy day, which only the thoughtless could neglect. All dark travail of soul, anguish or ecstasy of spirit, were hidden from her. If this moderation proceeded from magnanimity there would be nothing to object, but much to admire. But it proceeded from the opposite pole of moral endowment; from a cautious confined temper, incapable of self-forgetting ardour in any direction. Her maxim was never to quarrel with anybody, and she stoically adhered to it, under down-

D                                              treadings

treadings which would have caused a worm to turn. "Never boast," she says to her brother; "it is unlucky, and attracts ridicule." These words give the formula, as it were, from which her practical life was deduced. The meekness with which she carried her honours and supposed paramount influence rather puzzled the vainglorious world in which she moved. "I have seen her," says St. Simon, "yielding her place, and retreating everywhere before titled ladies; polite, affable, as a person who pretends to nothing, who makes a display of nothing, but who imposes much." The Scripture which says that he that exalteth himself shall be abased, she had taken thoroughly to heart: mingling therewith a flavour of the old Greek dread of a Nemesis awaiting the proud. Not to seize a high place, but to be invited to it, and again to retreat to a lower seat, flattered her delicate and fastidious self-love. She belongs to the class of "glorieuses modistes," as Ste. Beuve says, with untranslatable

latable felicity. It was this temper which has thrown such a pale grey hue over all her authentic letters. She never seems to write to anyone on anything out of fulness of heart. Almost without exception her letters are letters of business, written with a close practical object. In the fewest words and an Attic style she treats of the matter in hand. But all expansion of spirit or unburdening of heart are suppressed as if they were heresy or treason. One might suppose her letters were written under the impression that somebody was looking over her shoulder as she composed them.

With that perspicacity and talent of seeing things as they were, to which allusion has just been made, she saw this disposition in herself, and thus expressed it :—" My days are now spent in a regular course, and very solitary. I pray to God a moment on getting up. I go to two masses on days of obligation, and to one on other days. I say my office every day, and I read a chapter of some good book. I say my prayers on going

going to bed, and when I awake in the night I say a *Laudate* or a *Gloria Patri.* I often think of God in the daytime; I offer Him my actions; I beg He will take me from this (the court), if I cannot save my soul here; *and for the rest, I am not conscious of my sins. I have a morality and good inclinations which cause me to do scarcely any evil.* I have such a desire to please and to be liked, that I am on guard against my passions ; thus I never have to reproach myself with deeds, but with very worldly motives, a great vanity, much levity and dissipation, a great freedom in my thoughts and judgments, and carefulness in speech which is only founded on human prudence. This is about my state. Order the remedy which you think proper."[1] The self-knowledge here shown is remarkable, and the absence of cant admirable. The

---

* "Correspondance Générale," vol. i. page 96. "Du reste je ne connais pas mes péchés. J'ai une morale et de bonnes inclinations qui font que je ne fais guère de mal."

more singular is the cool self-possession of the passage and utter lack of all spiritual—we will not say fervour, but sensibility. Indeed. Madame de Maintenon's conscience was not easily alarmed, and when she had performed her regulation religious exercises and attended to her exchequer, she faced the future with serene outlook. She had a regrettable facility of seeing only one of these objects of her interest at a time, and the eye which observed her worldly concerns was perhaps more vigilant than its colleague which attended to spiritual matters. The years of contention with Montespan, and the humiliation they involved, already show this.

The gospel word that we cannot serve two masters must have seemed insipid to Madame de Maintenon, or at least it occasionally admitted of exceptions. She had brought the two services into complete agreement, or rather unity, and served Heaven most when she was performing her duties at court. But even she must

must have felt that now and again the combination was difficult. One cannot but lament that in 1677, when Madame de Montespan was again in a painfully interesting condition, and knew not where or how to escape from public observation, even as Aphrodite of old poured the obscurity of a welcome nimbus round her favourites, so Madame de Maintenon carried off the abashed, if not contrite, fair to her country house at Maintenon, and screened her for two months at a stretch from the prying gaze of a too curious world.[1] It is difficult to suppose that Christian charity alone operated here. The " terrible scenes " above alluded to had occurred two years before. The two ladies were on the terms fitting to the situation—shortly at daggers-drawn. Madame

---

* "À Maintenon ce 7 avril, 1677.—J'ai M. du Maine et Madame de Montespan ici, il y a six semaines." Again : "À Maintenon ce 8 mai, 1677.—J'ai toujours ici Madame de Montespan."—" Correspondance Générale," vol. i. pp. 329-332.

de

de Maintenon had prayed, and implored others to
pray, that she might be saved from the court and
its evil communications, and then takes the very
*corpus delicti* to her own home. Was this for edification? and if so, who was edified? It was not noble,
it was not even consistent. But undoubtedly circumstances were harsh and imperative. Even this
excuse cannot be pleaded, not for an action, but for
a thought, a suggestion of Madame de Maintenon to
her brother. That sorry spendthrift, for once, had a
little money, which his sister had procured for him
through a job with the farmers of the revenue. She
advised him, with her usual partiality for secure income, to lay it out in land in Poitou. "For," she
adds with complete coolness, "estates will be given
away there in consequence of the emigration of
the Protestants." Nothing recorded of Madame de
Maintenon gives us so unfavourable an impression of
her as this short sentence. She had tasted poverty,
and

and the shudder of it had never left her. She had been a Calvinist, and in a mild degree had suffered for her faith. But the anguish of that dread exodus passing under her eyes touched her not ; destitution and exile suffered for conscience' sake struck no chord of sympathy within her. The opportunity was favourable for a good investment. It seemed natural to her to seize it.[1]

The amount of influence exercised by Madame de Maintenon after her marriage with the King, has been a subject of much dispute from her own days to ours. Those who had forfeited or failed to win her favour, and who indemnified their overt adulation by secret calumny, ascribe every failure in war or policy to her sinister action. To St. Simon or La Princesse Palatine she is the evil principle of French

---

\* "Vous ne pourriez mieux faire que d'acheter une terre en Poitou ; elles vont s'y donner par la désertion des Huguenots." —"Correspondance Générale," vol. ii. p. 208.

politics,

politics, a mysterious shade gliding about the dark recesses of the court, touching and perverting every_ thing, but appearing frankly nowhere. Her admirers declared, and still declare, that her influence was powerless except for good. It is not very difficult to understand how these opposite impressions were produced. Madame de Maintenon's influence might easily be at once both very great and very limited; great in the dispensation of favours and promotions— a matter of supreme interest to the courtier world —and limited as to the great lines of policy pursued. The King's habit of working with his ministers in her cabinet, his occasional references to her, with the complimentary query, " What thinks your Solidity on this point ?" filled the troop of place-hunters with the alarmed conviction that her authority was paramount, and that one had to please her or die. When, again, we find her relating, with her usual proud humility, that her apartment was so full, that it was like a crowded

crowded church; that generals, ministers—nay, the
King's sons — waited in her ante-chamber till she
could receive them ; that the circle of ladies around
her was so close, that she could hardly breathe, we
may take it for granted that all this court was not
paid for nothing, and that that astute world knew
well what it was about when it took so much trouble.
On the other hand, she seems to have been not so
much incapable of, as profoundly indifferent to politics, which went nearer to boring her stoical patience
than perhaps anything else.  She lacked entirely the
intellectual audacity and ambition, the fervour and
freedom of spirit, which lead to bold political initia-
tive and courageous play for a great stake in that
high game.  And if she had had such qualities, we
may be quite sure she would not have been for long
a favourite of Louis XIV.

A less keen eye than hers would have measured
the robust stubbornness of the man, his morbid dread

of

of being ruled, and vanity so sensitive that no services, however long or valuable, failed to wound it.
She knew the fate of Colbert, of Louvois, and finally
of Montespan; and to leave no doubt on the
matter, she did make some timid attempts in the way
of direct influence, without success. " I did not
please in a conversation on the works now going
on, and my regret is to have given offence without
profit. Another building here will cost a hundred
thousand francs. Marly will soon be a second Versailles. There is no help for it but prayer and
patience." "The King will allow only his ministers
to talk to him about business. He took it ill that the
Nuncio addressed himself to me. I should be well
content with the life of slavery I lead if I could do
some good. I can only groan over the turn things
have taken." These avowals are made to an intimate
friend, Cardinal Noailles, Archbishop of Paris, and
cannot have been soothing to self-esteem. Then
contrast

contrast them with this report of an eye-witness :
"I have seen her sometimes when tired, vexed, dis-
quieted, and ill, assume the most smiling air and
cheerful tone, amuse the King by a thousand inven-
tions, entertain him alone four hours at a stretch,
without repetition, weariness, or scandal. When he
left her room at ten at night, and her bed-curtains
were being drawn, she would say to me with a sigh,
' I can only tell you that I am worn out.'" And yet
it is certain she had influence of no common kind.
It is in nowise surprising. The King's partiality for
her, which was such that he could not pass a quarter
of an hour in a crowded court without saying something in her ear—their unbroken intimacy and contact
for thirty years, must have given opportunities enough,
by the right word inserted in the right place, by the
well-chosen epithet attached to a name for honour or
disgrace, even by eloquent silence, to turn the scale
and make or mar the fortunes of soldier or civilian,

as

as the case might be. Thus her reputation is not much served by the distinction just made. After all, the selection of the *personnel* of a government is a highly important point, and it would seem that her action in this regard was on the whole injurious. Her partiality for Villeroi, Chamillart, and Voison cost France dear, if she had as much to do with their promotion as is alleged. On the other hand, let us honourably acquit her of the heavy charge of having urged the revocation of the Edict of Nantes, and the consequent persecutions. As far as she dared, her advice was given the other way, towards a mitigation of the severities exercised against the Huguenots; so much so, that the King said to her, "I fear, madame, that the mildness with which you would wish the Calvinists to be treated arises from some remaining sympathy with your former religion." It is, indeed, to her immense honour that she seems to have been entirely above the usual baseness of renegades, which leads

leads them to atone for their apostasy by calculated animosity and zeal against the communion they have left. The example of Pelisson showed her that such baseness was not without reward, but she remains free from all suspicion of it. Indeed, Madame de Maintenon's thoughts and interests were much less absorbed in the court than her enemies have supposed. Her heart was elsewhere—in her toy convent of St. Cyr.

St. Cyr took its origin in the quite laudable and benevolent wish to succour and relieve the daughters of noble houses of broken fortunes. She had been a well-born pauper and orphan, and determined to mitigate, to the limit of her power, the hard lot in others which she had felt so bitterly herself. She commenced in a humble way first at Rueil, and afterwards at Noisy. Lastly, she persuaded the King to erect the spacious building which still exists at St. Cyr, and endow it with 200,000 francs per annum. The conditions

ditions of admittance were poverty and noble birth The advantages offered were religious and practical education (especially needlework in all its branches was taught with great care), continued till the age of twenty, free of all cost or charge whatsoever; then a dowry or suitable marriage approved by the King, or a preferential nomination to places in religious houses in the gift of the Crown, when a vocation to the monastic life seemed manifest. The establishment consisted of two hundred and fifty pupils, governed by a staff of sixty nuns.

For the last thirty years of her life, Madame de Maintenon devoted all the time and thought she could save from her occupations at court to St. Cyr. Whenever she was residing at Versailles, she went at least every other day to her favourite institution, arriving there as early as six in the morning, and not returning till the same hour at night. She visited the classes and offices to see how the mistresses and
officers

officers performed their functions, inspected the infirmary, and often attended to and consoled the sick. When she had brought her establishment into something like working order, she persuaded the King to see it. The young ladies and their superiors received him, it need not be said, with all the grave pomp which became such a community. A *Te Deum* was sung, the damsels defiled before him, and each in passing made a profound reverence to his Majesty. Then, according to a tradition preserved at St. Cyr till its suppression, as he was about to enter the garden, a chorus of three hundred young voices greeted him with a hymn, of which the words were written by Madame de Brinon, the Mother Superior, and the music by Lulli. We seem to have heard the words before, though in another language :

> "Grand Dieu, sauvez le Roi !
> Grand Dieu, vengez le Roi !
> Vive le Roi !

Qu'à

Qu'à jamais glorieux,
Louis Victorieux,
   Voye ses ennemis,
   Toujours soumis,
Grand Dieu," &c., &c.

And not only the words, but the air, was exactly the same as our "God save the King." The French claim originality, and declare that Handel, who visited St. Cyr in 1721, stole the tune and took it with him to England. The English retort the charge of plagiarism. But if plagiarism there be, it seems more probable that a roving minstrel like Handel was able and willing to make the appropriation, than that a sedentary and secluded body like the ladies of St. Cyr should purloin from abroad a chant composed (on that supposition) in honour of a heretical prince —George I.

But soon St. Cyr was the scene of more festive entertainments. Madame de Maintenon thought that a little dramatic declamation might be at once

E                                                    an

an agreeable distraction and a useful exercise for her
young flock.  Some pieces of Corneille and Racine
were tried with only too much success.  They "contained passions dangerous for youth," and she wrote
to Racine—"Our little girls played yesterday your
*Andromaque,* and played it so well that they will play
it no more, nor any one of your pieces."  She then
asked the author of *Phèdre* if he could not write
something especially for St. Cyr, which would be
irreproachable on the score of dangerous passions.
After some hesitation he complied.  The result was
*Esther.*

Racine entered into his new occupation with much
interest, and even zeal.  He chose the most promis-
ing girls, and taught them their parts with much
assiduity.  At last the actresses were ready.  Persian
robes, trimmed with pearls and diamonds, had been
prepared, songs for the choruses composed, a tem-
porary theatre erected on the landing of the great
staircase.

staircase. After one or two rehearsals, Madame de Maintenon was satisfied with the effect, and determined to give the King a surprise. He came attended by only a few of the most intimate courtiers and bishops, and was so delighted with the play and spectacle, that when he got back to Versailles he did nothing but talk of *Esther.* The whole court, and even Paris, was forthwith seized with a perfect passion to see the new wonder. Nothing loth to renew an amusement in which he found so much pleasure, the King invited a larger circle of lords and ladies. This play-acting had now become serious business at St. Cyr, and while the teachers, assisted by Racine and Boileau, did their best to produce a result worthy of the occasion, it is not surprising that the " little novices" became, from excessive anxiety to acquit themselves well, not a little alarmed. Many of them, in their nervous fear of a breakdown, flung themselves on their knees before going on the stage, and repeated

peated a fervent *Veni Creator* to compose their spirits. The success was overwhelming. The rage to obtain admittance waxed ever hotter. Not only the usual courtiers, but the most grave bishops, the most learned magistrates, the most busy Ministers of State, struggled eagerly for a privilege which had now become a mark of signal favour. Bossuet went, and Father la Chaise, the King's confessor, and President Lamoignon. Madame de Sévigné could not get admitted till the fourth representation. The grandest display of all was on the 5th of February, 1689, when Louis took his royal guests, James II. and Mary of Modena, to see the play. He showed the exiles over the establishment with imperturbable urbanity, although James "appeared insensible to everything." The greatest order and decorum were observed on all occasions, in spite of the crowds. Madame de Maintenon had a list made out of those who were to be present, and strict orders were given to allow no

one

one to enter whose name did not appear in it. The King was early at his post, and seems to have voluntarily assumed the functions of boxkeeper. "When he arrived, he placed himself at the door inside, and holding up his cane to serve as a barrier, he remained till all those who were invited had entered. Then he caused the door to be shut. He permitted few of his suite to come in, and those who were admitted were ordered to be very silent, and not allowed to say a word to anybody." We may believe that Louis found more real enjoyment in these amusements, procured for him by his half-nun wife, than in the lavish galas and sumptuous ballets and carousals he had formerly given to please Madame de Montespan.

But this bright prospect was soon overcast. The ice once broken, the young performers took to their theatricals with such zest that they threatened to become actresses, and nothing else. The applause they

they had received puffed them up with vanity, and instead of a demure convent Madame de Maintenon found herself at the head of a troop of pert young ladies who thought only of pushing their fortunes at court, and of making good matches. Several did make conquests on the boards. A stringent reform was needed, and at last carried out with a great deal of trouble and anxiety to Madame de Maintenon. She acknowledged that she had been chiefly to blame for introducing a worldly spirit into the community. She was at one moment so disheartened that she was nearly disposed to throw up her undertaking. However, with time and patience she effected a thorough reformation. But this welcome result had hardly been achieved when a new peril assailed her from the opposite quarter. A morbid mysticism, introduced by the famous Madame Guyon, and propagated by Fénélon and Madame de la Maisonfort, filled St. Cyr with a heresy, and gave rise to much alarm in the orthodox

orthodox world all over France. That annoyance
was also subdued, but not until the brilliant author of
*Télémaque* had been disgraced by the King and con-
demned by the Pope, and the fascinating but rather
hysterical La Maisonfort and two other ladies of
St. Cyr had been removed out of harm's way by *lettre
de cachet* to a distance. Then at last Madame de
Maintenon had her toy convent all to herself. The
pleasure she had in going there, in dining with the
nuns and their pupils, is mentioned by her biogra-
phers, and referred to by herself with great unction,
as a proof apparently of singular spirituality of mind.
"As soon as she saw the towers of her dear Thebais,
of that abode of piety which God had given her to
restore her strength, she thanked Heaven." "When
I hear the door shut behind me on entering that
solitude, which I never leave without regret, I feel
full of joy." She seems indeed to have spent a good
portion of her time there in recounting with question-
able

able humility the fatigues and irritations of her life at court. " Oh, my dear daughters, how happy you are to have left the world, how happy to be occupied with God alone !" We must reconcile ourselves to this trait in Madame de Maintenon, to follow her own deepest inclination, and then to entreat pity for the sacrifice it involved. Assuredly she would not have been at court if she had not chosen to be there, and it is not wonderful that years of lassitude with the dreary and pompous etiquette of the court should have rendered the calm and repose of a religious house a welcome and refreshing change.

Madame de Maintenon, and the King also, rested great hopes on St. Cyr as a school of morals and piety, which would in time leaven all France. "There is enough there," she said, "to renew the perfection of Christianity in all the kingdom." He grew fonder of the place with advancing years and deepening religious convictions.   Often of an after-
noon,

noon, he would extend his walk to St. Cyr and hear vespers or compline in the convent chapel, after which the husband and wife would return home to Versailles in pensive mood, we may suppose. Louis was very gracious and even respectful to the nuns. If he happened to be in hunting dress he would not enter their holy precincts, but waited for Madame outside. At other times he would take one of the younger pupils on his knee (the age of admittance might be as low as seven), ask her name, and make her repeat her catechism. With the ladies who formed the religious staff, he conversed familiarly about the ordering of their house, and even about public affairs. Somebody spoke of founding another monastery. "There are other things much more urgent than that," said Madame de Maintenon, "to secure peace and relieve the poor people of their burdens." "Yes," said Louis, "that is what a king should aim at : peace in his kingdom, and relief of
his

his people.   But to obtain these advantages for them
we are forced against our will to oppress them.   We
want peace, but a good peace, and I ask it of God
continually."   "Who alone," added the King, "can
change the hearts of those who oppose it," viz., the
European coalition.   On one of these evenings at
St. Cyr, a skilful surprise was prepared for the King.
"It was on May 25th, 1704, after a soft spring day,
when the garden was in its beauty."   Louis XIV.
found all the young ladies with flowers in their hair,
grouped in bands, dancing and singing.   In his walk
at each avenue, each bosquet, he met one of these
joyous troops, from which children stepped out to
recite a dialogue or verses.   At last when the sun
was about to set behind the wooded hills of St. Cyr,
he stopped in the great parterre, whence can be seen
the magnificent view of the Val de Gallie, the park of
Versailles and the heights of the forest of Marly.
The damsels assembled round the ornamental piece
of

of water and sang a canticle, of which the first strophe was—

> " Du Seigneur troupes fidèles,
> Anges du ciel, veillez tous,
> Veillez, couvrez de vos ailes,
> Un roi qui veille sur nous." [1]

An idyllic scene, no doubt, but rather marred by an element which seems to come from the Opéra Comique.    Indeed, to enjoy it fully, we have need to forget the condition of France at the time.

Three ruinous wars, and a system more ruinous still of collecting the revenue which supported them, had brought France to the verge of exhaustion.    The population had greatly decreased all over the country —large towns, like Tours and Troyes, having lost two-thirds and three-fourths of their inhabitants. Commerce had declined in a similar ratio.    The silk

---

[1] " Madame de Maintenon et la Maison Royale de Saint-Cyr," p. 232.

manufacture

manufacture at Lyons had fallen since the prosperous days of Colbert from eighteen thousand to four thousand looms. The fisheries of Normandy and other trades had decayed largely. Not only the persecuted Huguenots, but other capitalists had emigrated, so insupportable was the onslaught of the great army of tax collectors let loose on the country by the farmers of the revenue. To the tillers of the soil, the worst lot, as ever, was reserved. They had already reached the *savage* state, subsequently described by the Marquis de Mirabeau, the Friend of Man, in the following century. "You may see troops of them," says the intendant of Bourges, "seated in a circle in the middle of a ploughed field, and always at a distance from the highways. If you approach, they disperse at once." Madame de Maintenon knew well the general misery from the condition of her own property. She wrote to her factor, "Give little in order to give to many. A good broth will nourish for
twenty-four

twenty-four hours. You have invention ; try whether peas, beans, milk, and barley-meal, or something, cannot replace bread, which is so dear." Worse still were the symptoms of fierce mistrust and hatred which crossed her path, the whole significance of which was not apparent to her as it is to us who know of '89. Daily she received letters asking her whether she was not tired of sucking the blood of the poor. In one of her journeys to St. Cyr, with her carriage full of food, clothing, and money, which she distributed to the famished crowd as she went along at a footpace, so great was the press, a child, half dead, was flung into her coach. Threats of assassination frequently reached her. " Matters have got to so violent a pitch that it cannot last," she writes. " You see people who will no longer listen to reason, and who are transported with misery. It will soon be impossible to go out with safety. The famine has put the people in such a ferment that one must not expose

expose oneself to it. The extremity is such that I am led to hope that God is about to interfere."

There is something touching as well as grotesque in this anticlimax. This was the result of forty years' reign by divine right, assisted by spiritual pastors even more divine. France had been given to the two heavenly-appointed authorities, as it were in the palms of their hands, to do what they would with her. All odious human liberty, corporate or individual, had been carefully extirpated as a poisonous weed. Parliaments, provincial estates, municipal liberties, had been suppressed with rigour. Religious dissent had been hunted down by dragoons, sword in hand. Calvinists, Quietists, Jansenists, had all in turn been persecuted with a ferocity which extorted the applause of all orthodox men, and placed Louis XIV. on a level with the greatest rulers of all time. Never had the principles of Catholic monarchy been put in practice on such a magnificent scale, with such unfettered

unfettered freedom, with such mature and wide deliberation. If the experiment did not succeed on these conditions, what conditions could be accounted sufficient? All that absolutism and intolerance could demand had been granted or taken. The issue was unsatisfactory in the extreme. Not only was heresy more daring and vigorous than ever abroad, but at home, in the heart of the country ruled by the most Christian King, civilization had stopped, or even retrograded. The population had diminished, the useful arts and agriculture were smitten with decay. A more beautiful example of the entire helplessness of Catholic monarchism before social problems has never been seen. Some distance across the Rhine there was a great Elector who, instead of impoverishing and half ruining a rich state, was building up an exhausted one with a success which astonished onlookers. Far off across the ocean, in the midst of primeval forests on the banks of the Delaware and

the

the Hudson, plain unpolished men were laying, with the success we know, the foundation of an empire destined to be the manifestation of principles the complete antithesis of those of the Grand Monarque.   The contrast is complete.

What strikes one most in the old French monarchy is not its abuses, injustices, cruelties, but its stupidity —its entire want of even enlightened self-interest. Not only did it never carry out any serious reform, it never fairly saw the need of any, and it turned fiercely on anyone who thought he did, *e.g.* Racine, Vauban, Boisguillebert and Fénélon.

It was a great trial to Madame de Maintenon that the King's conversion to a moral life almost coincided with the commencement of the misfortunes which filled the latter half of his reign.   We can understand her vexation.   That a licentious prince should be punished of God seemed to her a self-evident certainty.   That a chaste and pious prince
deserved

deserved Divine approval and reward was equally clear. But neither of these expectations was fulfilled. While Louis's life was a scandal and outrage to all decency, his arms and policy met with splendid success. After he had reformed and become a model to all Christian kings, had shown his devotion to God by private continency and public persecution, then he was afflicted in a manner which put faith at fault. " The King has changed his manner of living," writes the Abbé Dorat ; " he does secret penance, gives alms, makes long prayers, he insists that women shall be modestly dressed." The writer evidently feels he will hardly be believed. "The King has become a saint," he goes on ; " he has brought back to their duty several persons. He relieves secretly numbers of poor who are ashamed of their poverty, and regrets he has not always done so. He has such concern for virgin purity, that he takes elaborate measures to preserve it. All the ladies of the court

F have

have their necks and arms covered, so that nothing
but modesty is seen where they appear." If these
measures, these almost incredible reforms, will not
save a State, the question is what would? Madame
de Maintenon, at least, never doubted that God would
be at last touched by the piety of the King and the
prayer of her young ladies at St. Cyr. Whenever a
battle was expected, or a town besieged during the
disastrous war of the Spanish Succession, she prayed,
and made her young flock pray, with a fervency
which showed the stability of her faith. "The
prayers of forty hours were everywhere" when the
allies invested Lille. "The Duchess of Burgundy
passed nights in the chapel. Alarm was depicted in
every face, and this dread lasted nearly a month."
"The armies," she wrote, on the eve of Malplaquet,
"are confronting each other in Flanders. A courier
arrived with the news at five o'clock this morning.
Put all the house in prayer, I implore you, and go all

of

of you to offer the holy sacrifice to beseech God to protect us." Now and then, in her correspondence with the Princesse des Ursins, a flash of irritation escapes her at the obduracy of Heaven. "The designs of God are incomprehensible. Three Christian kings "—that is, Louis, the Pretender James III., and Philip V. of Spain—"appear to be abandoned, and heresy and injustice triumph. Let us hope that it will not be for long." It was not the first time, nor was it destined to be the last, that they who have taken the field with a firm conviction they had Providence for an ally have been exposed to disappointment. Marlborough was a heretic, and Eugene an infidel, and their victories over the forces of a pious and orthodox king were not only distressing to patriotism, but seemed to throw some discredit on the Divine verities of faith. More dismal years there are not in history than those which closed the long and once brilliant reign of Louis XIV. The savage war,

war, waged with half-starved troops, led by incompe-
tent generals; the silent anguish of the provinces
which seemed to fall asleep, numbed in misery; the
lugubrious pomp of Versailles, in which the failing
old King moved like a spectre seeking rest—form a
picture as sombre as can well be conceived. The
terrible winter of 1709-10, in which half the fruit
trees perished, and which human and animal life with
difficulty survived, seems like a metaphor offered by
nature of the dark cold gloom which had settled on
the land, stagnating the blood and the minds of men.
The frightful silence is only pierced by the strident
voices of theological disputants, like jackals on a battle-
field, active and hungry in the midst of death.

Louis met his death, as he had his misfortunes,
with more courage than might have been expected of
him. "I thought," he said to Madame de Maintenon, "I thought it had been more difficult to die."
The frost of old age was congealing them both. He
was

was seventy-seven, and she eighty years old. Much has been related of doubtful truth concerning her forsaking him in his last moments. She no doubt did leave him and go to St. Cyr on the 28th of August, that is, two days before he died. But he had become unconscious, and no one expected he would revive. When he did, she was at his bedside at once. "You must have much fortitude," he said to her, "to be always present at such a spectacle." They had bidden each other farewell some days before in terms of real affection. If their words seem wanting in lofty human passion, we must remember the persons and the circumstances.

Madame de Maintenon lived four years at St. Cyr after Louis XIV.'s death. She not only received numerous messages of sympathy from the chief persons at court, but the Regent Duke of Orleans hastened to pay her a visit of condolence. He not only confirmed to her her modest pension of 48,000 francs

francs a year (Madame de Montespan had been known to lose fifteen times that sum in a bet on a single card), but he declared to her detractors, " She did good to everybody as much as she could, and never did harm to anyone." The most generous (and not wholly undeserved) tribute ever made to Madame de Maintenon.

www.ingramcontent.com/pod-product-compliance
Lightning Source LLC
Chambersburg PA
CBHW031449270326
41930CB00007B/925